Fertility of Malian Tamasheq Repatriated Refugees

The Impact of Forced Migration

Sara Randall

Roundtable on the Demography of Forced Migration
Committee on Population

NATIONAL RESEARCH COUNCIL
OF THE NATIONAL ACADEMIES

and
Program on Forced Migration and Health at the
Mailman School of Public Health
Columbia University

D1361803

THE NATIONAL ACADEMIES PRESS
Washington, DC
www.nap.edu

THE NATIONAL ACADEMIES PRESS   500 Fifth Street, N.W.   Washington, DC 20001

NOTICE: The project that is the subject of this report was approved by the Governing Board of the National Research Council, whose members are drawn from the councils of the National Academy of Sciences, the National Academy of Engineering, and the Institute of Medicine. The members of the committee responsible for the report were chosen for their special competences and with regard for appropriate balance.

This study was supported by grants to the National Academy of Sciences and the Mailman School of Public Health of Columbia University by the Andrew W. Mellon Foundation. Any opinions, findings, conclusions, or recommendations expressed in this publication are those of the authors and do not necessarily reflect the view of the organizations or agencies that provided support for this project.

International Standard Book Number 0-309-09238-8 (Book)
International Standard Book Number 0-309-53278-7 (PDF)

Additional copies of this report are available from the National Academies Press, 500 Fifth Street, N.W., Lockbox 285, Washington, DC 20055; (800) 624-6242 or (202) 334-3313 (in the Washington metropolitan area); Internet, http://www.nap.edu

Printed in the United States of America.

Suggested citation: National Research Council. (2004). *Fertility of Malian Tamasheq Repatriated Refugees: The Impact of Forced Migration.* Sara Randall. Roundtable on the Demography of Forced Migration. Committee on Population, Division of Behavioral and Social Sciences and Education and Program on Forced Migration and Health at the Mailman School of Public Health of Columbia University. Washington, DC: The National Academies Press.

THE NATIONAL ACADEMIES
Advisers to the Nation on Science, Engineering, and Medicine

The **National Academy of Sciences** is a private, nonprofit, self-perpetuating society of distinguished scholars engaged in scientific and engineering research, dedicated to the furtherance of science and technology and to their use for the general welfare. Upon the authority of the charter granted to it by the Congress in 1863, the Academy has a mandate that requires it to advise the federal government on scientific and technical matters. Dr. Bruce M. Alberts is president of the National Academy of Sciences.

The **National Academy of Engineering** was established in 1964, under the charter of the National Academy of Sciences, as a parallel organization of outstanding engineers. It is autonomous in its administration and in the selection of its members, sharing with the National Academy of Sciences the responsibility for advising the federal government. The National Academy of Engineering also sponsors engineering programs aimed at meeting national needs, encourages education and research, and recognizes the superior achievements of engineers. Dr. Wm. A. Wulf is president of the National Academy of Engineering.

The **Institute of Medicine** was established in 1970 by the National Academy of Sciences to secure the services of eminent members of appropriate professions in the examination of policy matters pertaining to the health of the public. The Institute acts under the responsibility given to the National Academy of Sciences by its congressional charter to be an adviser to the federal government and, upon its own initiative, to identify issues of medical care, research, and education. Dr. Harvey V. Fineberg is president of the Institute of Medicine.

The **National Research Council** was organized by the National Academy of Sciences in 1916 to associate the broad community of science and technology with the Academy's purposes of furthering knowledge and advising the federal government. Functioning in accordance with general policies determined by the Academy, the Council has become the principal operating agency of both the National Academy of Sciences and the National Academy of Engineering in providing services to the government, the public, and the scientific and engineering communities. The Council is administered jointly by both Academies and the Institute of Medicine. Dr. Bruce M. Alberts and Dr. Wm. A. Wulf are chair and vice chair, respectively, of the National Research Council.

www.national-academies.org

ROUNDTABLE ON THE DEMOGRAPHY OF
FORCED MIGRATION
2004

CHARLES B. KEELY *(Chair)*, Walsh School of Foreign Service, Georgetown University

LINDA BARTLETT, Division of Reproductive Health, Centers for Disease Control and Prevention, Atlanta

RICHARD BLACK, Center for Development and Environment, University of Sussex

STEPHEN CASTLES, Refugee Studies Centre, University of Oxford

WILLIAM GARVELINK, Bureau of Humanitarian Response, U.S. Agency for International Development, Washington, DC

ANDRE GRIEKSPOOR, Emergency and Humanitarian Action Department, World Health Organization, Geneva

JOHN HAMMOCK, Feinstein International Famine Center, Tufts University

BELA HOVY, Population Data Unit, United Nations High Commissioner for Refugees, Geneva

JENNIFER LEANING, School of Public Health, Harvard University

NANCY LINDBORG, Mercy Corps, Washington, DC

CAROLYN MAKINSON, Andrew W. Mellon Foundation, New York

SUSAN F. MARTIN, Institute for the Study of International Migration, Georgetown University

W. COURTLAND ROBINSON, Center for Refugee and Disaster Studies, Johns Hopkins University

SHARON STANTON RUSSELL, Center for International Studies, Massachusetts Institute of Technology

WILLIAM SELTZER, Department of Sociology and Anthropology, Fordham University

PAUL SPIEGEL, United Nations High Commissioner for Refugees, Geneva

RONALD J. WALDMAN, Joseph L. Mailman School of Public Health, Columbia University

ANTHONY ZWI, School of Public Health and Community Medicine, University of New South Wales

Staff

BARNEY COHEN, *Director, Committee on Population*

ANA-MARIA IGNAT, *Senior Program Assistant*

v

Preface

In response to the need for more research on displaced persons, the Committee on Population developed the Roundtable on the Demography of Forced Migration in 1999. This activity, which is supported by the Andrew W. Mellon Foundation, provides a forum in which a diverse group of experts can discuss the state of knowledge about demographic structures and processes among people who are displaced by war and political violence, famine, natural disasters, or government projects or programs that destroy their homes and communities. The roundtable includes representatives from operational agencies, with long-standing field and administrative experience. It includes researchers and scientists with both applied and scholarly expertise in medicine, demography, and epidemiology. The group also includes representatives from government, international organizations, donors, universities, and nongovernmental organizations.

The roundtable is organized to be as inclusive as possible of relevant expertise and to provide occasions for substantive sharing to increase knowledge for all participants, with a view toward developing cumulative facts to inform policy and programs in complex humanitarian emergencies. To this aim, the roundtable has held annual workshops on a variety of topics, including mortality patterns in complex emergencies, demographic assessment techniques in emergency settings, and research ethics among conflict-affected and displaced populations.

Another role for the roundtable is to serve as a promoter of the best research in the field. The field is rich in practitioners but is lacking a coherent body of research. Therefore the roundtable and the Program on Forced Migration and Health at the Mailman School of Public Health of Columbia University have established a monograph series to promote research on various aspects of the demography of forced migration. These occasional monographs are individually authored documents presented to the roundtable and any recommendations or conclusions are solely attributable to the authors. It is hoped these monographs will result in the formulation of newer and more scientifically sound public health practices and policies and will identify areas in which new research is needed to guide the development of forced migration policy.

This monograph was prepared for and presented at the Workshop on Fertility and Reproductive Health in Complex Humanitarian Emergencies held in October 2002.

This monograph has been reviewed in draft form by individuals chosen for their diverse perspectives and technical expertise in accordance with procedures approved by the National Research Council's Report Review Committee. The purpose of this independent review is to provide candid and critical comments that will assist the institution in making the published monograph as accurate and as sound as possible. The review comments and draft manuscript remain confidential.

Ronald J. Waldman of Columbia University served as review coordinator for this report. We wish to thank the following individuals for their participation in the review of this report: Parfait Eloundou-Enyegue of the Department of Development Sociology and the Population and Development Program at Cornell University; Thérèse Locoh of INED Paris; and David Shapiro of the Department of Economics, Pennsylvania State University.

Although the individuals listed above provided constructive comments and suggestions, it must be emphasized that responsibility for this monograph rests entirely with the authors.

This series of monographs is being made possible by a special collaboration between the Roundtable on the Demography of Forced Migration of The National Academies and the Program on Forced Migration and Health at the Mailman School of Public Health of Columbia University. We thank the Andrew W. Mellon Foundation for its continued support of the work of the roundtable and the program at Columbia. A special thanks is due Carolyn Makinson of the Mellon Foundation for her enthusiasm and significant expertise in the field of forced migration, which she has shared with the roundtable, and for her help in facilitating partnerships such as this.

Most of all, we are grateful to the author of this monograph. We hope that this publication contributes to both better policy and better practice in the field.

Charles B. Keely, *Chair*
Roundtable on the Demography of Forced Migration

Ronald J. Waldman, *Member*
Roundtable on the Demography of Forced Migration and Director, Program on Forced Migration at the Mailman School of Public Health of Columbia University

Contents

Fertility of Malian Tamasheq Repatriated Refugees: The Impact of Forced Migration

FERTILITY AND FORCED MIGRATION

In Africa many of the refugee flows in recent years have had a strong ethnic dimension; interethnic conflict or conflict between politically powerful groups with minority populations is often an important aspect of who is forced to flee. In most cases the origins of conflict occur in a multiethnic environment, and repatriation (if it happens) occurs in that multiethnic context, with implications for subsequent relationships between the groups in terms of political, economic, and numeric power. As the primary source of recruitment to a population, fertility is an essential component of postconflict restructuring. The disruption of fertility during the disorder of forced migration can itself be seen as part of the disintegration of society and identity; the impact of conflict and flight on reproduction may be an important indicator of the degree of crisis faced by the population. Postcrisis fertility and changes from the reproductive regime prior to the forced migration indicate not only how the population has responded to the multiplicity of changes and traumas, but also its ability to adapt and manipulate its new sociopolitical position.

Studies of the impact of forced migration on fertility in developing countries are rare, although more are available on the impact of famine and war on fertility. The study by Agadjanian and Prata (2002) of Angolan fertility in high conflict and interconflict periods shows declines in birth probabilities when conflict was intense and a rebound in fertility during more peaceful interludes. The declines were most marked for the urban populations who, although not necessarily exposed to most conflict, through more use of fertility control had more potential for adjusting fertility behavior in response to periods of stress and uncertainty. The data used for this Angolan study excluded refugee camp populations and thus may have minimized the impact of forced migration on fertility, focusing more on general consequences of conflict. The study by Lindstrom and Berhanu (1999) of the impact of war, famine, and economic decline on national and regional marital fertility in Ethiopia considered only four residential categories (one urban and three rural areas), so any differential responses of particular ethnic subpopulations were masked.

In Africa ethnic identity is frequently an important determinant of rural fertility regimes (Brass et al., 1968; Randall, 1984; Lestaeghe, 1989), but national-level data may mask any ethnicity-specific fertility consequences of conflict and forced migration. This is a substantial analytical problem given ethnic heterogeneity and the variable sociopolitical roles and positions of particular ethnic groups in many conflicts. Whereas several studies have considered the general role of war, economic insecurity, and famine on fertility (National Research Council, 2004), few have focused on the specific experience of a single persecuted population whose sociopolitical history, along with their underlying marital and fertility regimes, will inevitably condition responses to conflict. Outside Africa, the exceptional case of the Palestinians demonstrates a pronounced fertility response to that particular drawn-out refugee crisis in its specific political context, with fertility being substantially higher than would be expected from the level of socioeconomic development (Courbage, 1995; Khawaja, 2000; Pedersen, Randall, and Khawaja, 2001).

From studies of both conflict and famine in populations in which fertility control is widespread, it is clear that there is a short- and medium-term impact on fertility, largely mediated through conscious decisions not to reproduce, probably coupled with reductions in coital frequency and increases in spousal separation (see National Research Council, 2004). The impacts of malnutrition and stress on fecundity cannot be ruled out. The responses of rural populations with natural fertility are less well documented; both the Angolan and Ethiopian studies cited above show the most effects of conflict and crisis on the urban population, for which fertility control was most widespread. It is therefore important to examine the impacts of forced migration on noncontracepting populations in order to understand the potential for conflict to disrupt and transform reproduction, but to do this, data are needed on the preconflict fertility regime. Malian Kel Tamasheq, many of whom fled violence and Mali to live in refugee camps for several years in the 1990s, are a rural, noncontracepting population for whom such pre- and postconflict data are available.

BACKGROUND

Kel Tamasheq[1] live across Northern Mali, southern Algeria, Niger, and northern Burkina Faso. Most used to be archetypal nomadic pastoralists, herding goats, sheep, cattle, and camels, according to the local environment. Two populations of nomadic pastoralist Kel Tamasheq were studied in 1981 and 1982 (Randall, 1984, 1996).

The delta Tamasheq at that time spent the dry season using pastures in the inner Niger delta,[2] leaving in the wet season to move north and west into drier areas, such as the Mema—the semi-arid area to the west of the Niger delta—and toward Tombouctou (see map). This pattern of movement itself was relatively recent, with the Kel Tamasheq first entering the inner Niger delta in substantial numbers after the 1913 drought. Most of these delta Tamasheq were from the Cherifen and Kel Antessar confederations of warrior marabouts. The Gourma Tamasheq[3] living south of the Niger bend, studied in 1982, included more of the vassal class and lower status free Kel Tamasheq; both areas were socially heterogeneous, with representatives of all the different Tamasheq social classes: warriors, religious maraboutic groups, vassals, lower status groups, blacksmiths, and slaves and ex-slaves.

---

[1]The Kel Tamasheq are the people who speak Tamasheq, a Berber language. Some Tamasheq-speaking groups are also known as Tuareg.

[2]In the dry Sahel with its limited seasonal rainfall, the inner Niger delta flood plain and river system are an extremely valuable source of water for both pasture and agriculture. It is an ethnically heterogenous zone dominated both economically and politically by Peul agropastoralists, who are the traditional managers of access to both land and pastures. Many other groups use the delta resources either seasonally or permanently, including Bozo transhumant fishers, Somono river transporters, and different groups of agriculturalists and herders.

[3]In this paper no data are presented from the Gourma survey because the 2001 study did not restudy these groups— who mainly took refuge in Burkina Faso during the rebellion. However the Gourma Tamasheq in the early 1980s had an almost identical demographic regime to the Delta Tamasheq including the social class mortality differentials, relatively low fertility and a similar marriage regime.

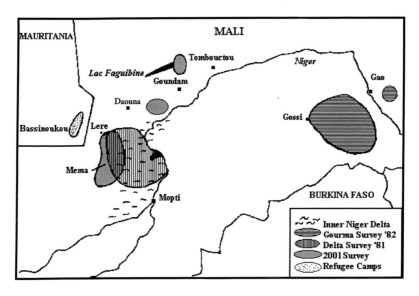

Other pastoralist populations, such as Maures, Arabs, and Fulani, also exploit the Gourma pastures, and most groups have some traditional rights over access to the River Niger for water and pastures. All along the river there are Songhay villages practicing various forms of flood retreat and irrigated agriculture.

In precolonial times there were close economic and commercial links between the different pastoralist and agricultural groups in the area, since each needs the products, resources, and skills of the other. According to Marty (1999), as part of their attempts to control the Kel Tamasheq, the French tried to sever and disrupt these links with long-term deleterious consequences, since "survival was only possible with human groups from different societies endowed with both human and natural resources allowing complementary subsistence strategies, starting with grain and livestock. In this Sahelien environment, where resources vary considerably over time and space, stability is only possible with systems which allow adjustments and exchange of services between ethnic groups and between different economic activities which are each essential for the other" (p. 290, author's translation).

Thus in both areas the Kel Tamasheq have long been part of a multiethnic environment with considerable contacts and interdependencies between different groups.

Tamasheq warriors, maraboutic classes, and vassals, along with some other lower status free Kel Tamasheq, are all descended from Arab and Berber populations who crossed the Sahara, probably in the 15th and 16th centuries. Tamasheq is a Berber language; physically most higher status Kel Tamasheq are fair-skinned North Africans and are variously referred to both by themselves and other Malians as red (rouges) or white (blanches). The warrior class (a tiny minority) were also called Tuareg and in recent years this nomenclature has been extended in Mali to refer to all the higher status fair-skinned Kel Tamasheq.

As in many West African communities, slavery was a well-established institution in precolonial times, and most Kel Tamasheq slaves (iklan or Bella[4]) were originally captured in raids on villages and other communities living in these ethnically mixed areas. Bella are black African and speak Tamasheq, yet they clearly have genetic origins different from the Berber Tamasheq. Although many slaves were liberated in the colonial period and after independence, de facto ownership of slaves still continued at the time of the 1981-1982 surveys, with many high-status Tamasheq having resident Bella to do most domestic and herding work. The 1981-1982 surveys included both these domestic Bella and Bella who had been freed for several generations.[5]

Another group of Bella, not studied in 1981-1982, are sedentary sharecroppers who work the fields owned by some Tuareg, particularly lands around Lake Faguibine. Few, if any, of the Tuareg surveyed in 1981-1982 actually used sharecropping, getting most of their grain from the sale of animals, from gathering wild grains, or from their Bella who used to work

---

[4]The Tamasheq word for the slave class, iklan, is a term with pejorative overtones. In Mali, this group of black Tamasheq slaves and ex-slaves is generally known by the Songhay term Bella, which I use here. There are many different categories of Bella; some were liberated by their masters generations ago, some were liberated by the French, and others left their masters when successive laws abolished slavery. Gradual impoverishment of Malian Kel Tamasheq in recent decades has resulted in many Bella leaving the pastoral sector altogether.

[5]In this paper I use the term Tuareg to refer to the higher status, fair-skinned Berber population and Bella for the black African ex-slaves. In the rebellion only the Tuareg were persecuted and forced to flee. Ideally, demographic analysis would also distinguish blacksmiths, who are a separate class of free Tamasheq, but their numbers are too small. Because this class is also black African, because they were not persecuted, and because their women have always been very economically active, they are included in the Bella category for all the analyses below.

on the harvest for other populations in the area. Other groups of Malian Tuareg received (and receive) substantial amounts of grain from their fields—usually worked by Bella.

Blacksmiths are an endogamous caste group who traditionally made and repaired all the metal, wooden, and leather articles in return for which they received milk, grain, cash, and protection. Blacksmith families were usually attached to a Tuareg patron with whom they transhumed (i.e., moving with livestock on a circuit following seasonally available pastures), although many have now moved to villages or towns, where they sell their goods in the markets.

French colonial perceptions were largely responsible for the well-established idea that Tuareg had low fertility (Gallais, 1975), and the French also thought that Bella had low fertility. Low fertility was confirmed by the 1980s surveys, which showed the Kel Tamasheq (both Tuareg and Bella) studied to be demographically unusual for Sub-Saharan African populations. Heterogeneity in terms of production, environment, and social organization in the Kel Tamasheq population in Mali means that one cannot generalize about all Malian Kel Tamasheq demography; still, some of the specifics almost certainly apply elsewhere. The demographic regime was typified by relatively low fertility,[6] largely a function of the nuptiality regime, and unusual patterns of mortality differentials. Higher status (and usually wealthier) Tuareg children had much higher mortality than low-status blacksmith and Bella children (Hill and Randall, 1984). In both the delta and the Gourma, Tuareg women had higher mortality than blacksmith and Bella women, but the opposite was the case for adult men. Although extramarital childbearing was more acceptable for Bella, overall their total fertility was similar to that of the Tuareg (Randall and Winter, 1985).

This demographic regime has been interpreted largely as a consequence of cultural values, in which the economic and social role of women had a major impact on demographic outcomes (Randall, 1984; Fulton and Randall, 1988). In these two regions, Tuareg women were traditionally respected in the home and expected to do little domestic work; this was possible because of the dependent slave population. Class-based behavioral differences were reinforced by force-feeding many rich Tuareg girls and young women; subsequent obesity meant that many were physically unable

---

[6]Total fertility rate between 5 and 6 compared with over 7 for other rural Malian populations.

to do much work. The population is monogamous despite being Muslim, and women rarely accepted co-wives, threatening to leave the marriage if their husbands attempted polygamy. Tuareg women contributed little to the household economy; would demand food, goods, and material things from their husbands;[7] and often did little active child care. Given that there were no effective health services to mediate between a child's illness and death other than the daily care the child received, child care patterns are thought to have been largely responsible for the differential mortality rates between social classes (Hill and Randall, 1984).

There was, however, substantial diversity over both space and time. The extent of both force-feeding and slavery had been declining for at least two decades before the 1981-1982 demographic surveys, but in the populations studied they were still quite frequent. In some areas of Mali, Kel Tamasheq had become less nomadic as a consequence of herd loss in the 1973 drought; simultaneously there was a decline in the domestic slave population, with Bella either moving to urban areas or becoming independent herders. Although some urban Kel Tamasheq were highly educated, in the two populations studied in 1981-1982 everyone was nomadic, few had been to modern school,[8] and there was little contact with modern health services. Most people lived in relatively small, isolated camps (20-40 people). Men had contact with the outside world through travel and movement to markets, and most women led very restricted lives.

A major drought in 1985 led to substantial herd losses, population movements, food aid, and a mushrooming of international and local nongovernmental organizations (NGOs). Dependent Bella left their owners, people moved temporarily to the towns, and some groups started to sedentarize—that is, abandon the highly mobile, nomadic lifestyle (Randall and Giuffrida, 2003). Those who remained nomadic became less isolated, with increased knowledge about the outside world and contact with development projects.

In 1990 rebellion broke out first in Niger and was followed by an attack in east Mali. Thereafter small bands of armed Tuareg attacked military and administrative posts, sometimes killing the incumbents, usually stealing vehicles. The MPLA (Mouvement Populaire pour la Libération de

---

[7]Miscarriage is believed to be provoked by a woman wanting something she can't have.

[8]Only one woman of the 3,000 interviewed could speak French; she was an interviewer in the 2001 study.

l'Azawad) was created with the aim of liberating Tuareg territories in the north. The Malian army responded at first by patrolling the areas and then clashed with the rebels. Despite negotiations mediated by the Algerians, the rebel attacks increased in intensity throughout early 1991 and gradually expanded westward toward Tombouctou and the Mema. As the rebel attacks increased, so did those of the Malian army on both Tuareg and Maures, and men, women, and children were killed in several camps and communities. The general Malian population became incited against the "reds," and there were popular attacks and raids against shops owned by Tuareg and Maures throughout northern and central Mali. Skin color and physical appearance were major factors identifying those who were attacked; after the "massacre de Lere" in May 1991, Tuareg in the Niger delta and the Mema areas started to flee en masse to Mauritania[9] (elsewhere people fled to Algeria, Niger, and Burkina Faso) just across the border. Some took their herds and tried to continue to be nomadic pastoralists in Mauritania, although they faced major problems with access to water and wells; some consumed many of their animals en route; others left everything behind.

The United Nations High Commissioner for Refugees (UNHCR), the World Food Programme, and various NGOs responded rapidly to the huge influx of people, and three refugee camps were set up just inside Mauritania. Conditions were poor at first because of the scale of the crisis and the isolation of the area, which was several hours' rough drive from Mauritania's main arterial road. People continued to flood into the refugee camps through 1991 and 1992 and into 1993. The majority stayed until 1996, although spontaneous repatriations and movements away from the camps occurred throughout the period. Nevertheless, the main waves into the Mauritanian refugee camps occurred in 1991, and the main wave out occurred in 1996 under a repatriation program run by UNHCR and the German Agency for Technical Cooperation (GTZ) after the signing of various peace agreements. Many people spent about 4 or 5 years in the refugee camps.

Although the majority of camp residents had previously been nomadic pastoralists, there were also people who had sedentarized after the 1985 drought, along with Kel Tamasheq and Maure civil servants, teachers, trad-

---

[9]Most people in the Mema left because there was nowhere there to hide. Further north, around Goundam and Tombouctou, some fled but others hid with their animals in the mountains and the desert.

ers, craftsmen, and students—people who would normally have had limited contact with the nomadic pastoralists either professionally or during holidays. A few Bella and blacksmiths fled with their patrons, but Bella were not persecuted and many stayed behind, some with the animals, some leaving the pastoral sector altogether.

For the nomadic pastoralist majority, there were many changes brought about by being in the refugee camps, including being fixed in one place with many people from other social groups, other lineages, and those who had been educated and had moved outside the pastoral sector and zone. This led to a huge scope for a substantial social life, particularly for young people. Rudimentary health care provisions developed into immunization programs and free health and maternity care. Whereas previously nomadic delta Kel Tamasheq drank water from marshes and the river, boreholes now provided clean tap water. In later years, schools were set up in the refugee camps, and some women received training to facilitate economic independence after repatriation.

The numbers of people in the three refugee camps[10] fluctuated over time, and there are no precise estimates. There is evidence that in the early period the numbers were considerably inflated in order to receive more per capita rations. Anecdotal evidence also suggests that some local Mauritanians moved into the camps in order to benefit from resources. UNHCR data on repatriation (Sperl, 2000) indicates that 43,712 individuals (both Tamasheq and Maure) were repatriated between 1995 and 1997, suggesting that the camps may have contained rather more than this at their peak. NGOs estimated that about 55,000 people were in the refugee camps in 1995, of whom about 65 percent were Tamasheq (ACORD et al., 1995). The situation of high numbers of people settled in close proximity to each other was substantially different from the previous low-density mobile lifestyle. There were other Tamasheq in Mauritania during the conflict—people who went directly to cities, some who formed small unofficial camps, some who transhumed around the refugee camps and who had close kin in the camps—maintaining the tradition of using mobility and diversification to maximize resources.

---

[10]The three camps were all within about 30 kilometers of each other, close to the Mali-Mauritania frontier, and remote from any Mauritanian infrastructure. A fourth camp was opened when one of the others was closed. In the camps, people were organized into quartiers or districts, each of which had an appointed chief as representative.

Repatriation made further changes to lifestyle. Part of the repatriation package presented by UNHCR included promises to build schools, drill wells, and help develop infrastructure in the specific destinations that refugees were obliged to name and return to. This encouraged sedentarization and has led to a proliferation of wells surrounded by small settlements (Randall and Giufrrida, 2003). People with few or no animals (and many people had lost most of their animals) no longer needed to be mobile, and many of those who retained animals claimed now to have seen the benefits of a stationary lifestyle. This sedentarization was compounded by pressure from women who, without domestic labor, would have to do all the pitching and striking of nomadic camps themselves.

Thus, after repatriation, much of the population is sedentarized, fewer are totally dependent on a pastoral economy, there is little unpaid domestic labor available, and women are thinner. Very fat women suffered terribly during the flight, and there is now a consensus that substantial obesity poses problems in times of insecurity. Not only are there no longer the resources and milk surpluses to force-feed girls, but also the majority of girls no longer wish to be extremely fat. Other changes include an increased acceptability of education for both boys and girls; increased knowledge about and demand for modern health services; better quality water, which is usually also close at hand; changing domestic roles of women, who now have to do more work in the household; and increased acceptability and willingness to undertake agriculture. The population is more highly politicized and feels vulnerable about being physically conspicuous in Mali, with many believing there could be future violence against them.

STUDYING THE IMPACTS OF
FORCED MIGRATION ON FERTILITY

In examining the various stages of fertility-related repercussions of forced migration, it is essential to consider the context of preconflict patterns of reproduction, attitudes to fertility, determinants of fertility, and perception of the reproduction of both one's own group and neighboring populations, particularly when they too were involved in the conflict. Figure 1 outlines a framework for considering these stages of the forced migration process and speculates about the differing weight of fertility determinants at each stage.

Three basic periods of forced migration can be identified, although each specific situation has its own complexities and modifications. *Disorder*

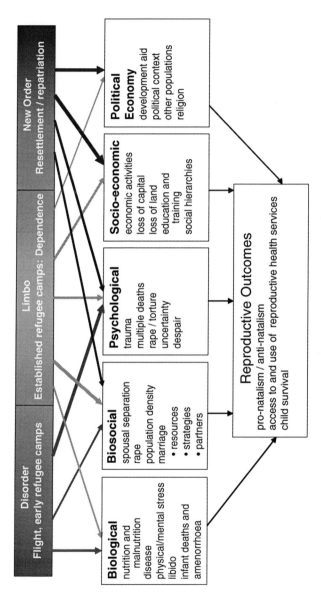

FIGURE 1 Conceptualization of phases of forced migration and impacts on fertility.

includes the period of flight and movement and the early phases of adaptation to life in a different environment, often in temporary camps of some kind. The second phase, *limbo,* is the period of exile when immediate danger is past but people are not yet in a position to begin to rebuild their lives. In many situations, this will be in refugee camps supported by UNHCR and NGOs. The basic logistical problems of health care and sanitation have often been resolved, but generally people are economically dependent on outside aid and resources. Although there may be limited economic activity, particularly trade, there is rarely any primary production and most people are spatially and economically in limbo. This phase may be very short or may last for many years; one could argue that many Palestinians have spent half a century in this position. The final phase, *new order,* is the rebuilding of a "normal" independent economic life contingent on resettlement or repatriation.

In each phase of forced migration, fertility is likely to be influenced by many voluntary and involuntary forces. Although particular situations and individual cases will always be subject to different influences, they can be grouped broadly into five categories (see Figure 1), each of which will have a different degree of importance (in terms of impact on precrisis fertility norms) in the three phases of the forced migration crisis (represented by the thickness of the arrows).

For example, during the period of disorder, the biological impacts will often resemble those in famine situations: nutritional crisis, disease, stress, loss of libido, possibly counteracted slightly by infant deaths and curtailed breast-feeding (Ashton et al., 1984; Watkins and Menken, 1985; Dyson, 1991). Biosocial impacts on fertility will be a consequence of spousal separation (possibly counteracted by rape), population density, and lack of privacy. Psychological factors are also likely to have a major impact on reproductive behavior at this stage.

In the period of limbo, all five types of influence are likely to operate, although with different intensities (and different outcomes) according to the particularities of the situation; biosocial and psychological factors usually being more important than biological or those of the political economy. The latter, along with socioeconomic impacts, will probably dominate fertility behavior in the new order. Clearly all impacts on fertility in each of the phases will have to operate through the proximate determinants of fertility, but it is more helpful to think of the wider scenarios influencing these responses.

An alternative perspective of the consequences of forced migration on fertility is to consider crisis-related changes that have a *direct* impact on fertility (including most of the biological and biosocial factors and some of the psychological ones) and those that have an *indirect* impact—for example, socioeconomic changes modifying some of the proximate determinants of fertility, often the marriage regime. A third level of change is that of *conscious demographic manipulation;* its strategies emerge either as a response to the threats that originally led to exile or as a form of insurance against renewed persecution.

These two frameworks for conceptualizing the impact of forced migration on fertility and reproductive health are used in this paper to examine the case of the Kel Tamasheq in western Mali. Given the Tamasheq demographic regime in 1981, ethnographic knowledge of this population, and objective observations of both their demographic position relative to other Malian populations, combined with the substantial socioeconomic changes undergone during and after exile, one would predict substantial changes in fertility as a consequence of the forced migration experience. I consider the degree to which there is evidence that the three phases identified in the framework do actually reflect different fertility behavior and which proximate determinants seem to be most susceptible to change in this conflict. By comparing those who lived in the refugee camps with the smaller numbers of people who remained in Mali during the conflict, the particular role of such lifestyle transformations on reproduction can be examined, focusing in particular on subtle changes in marriage patterns. In consideration of any changes observed in nuptiality, one must always bear in mind the possibility of conscious demographic manipulation, since pronatalist strategies must be considered as a possible response to perceived vulnerability consequent upon repatriation into an ethnically heterogeneous environment.

Methods

In 1981 we attempted to survey all Kel Tamasheq who spent the dry season transhuming in the inner Niger delta. The survey was undertaken at the end of the dry season, when people are most grouped together (Randall, 1984); it was a single-round retrospective survey in which we also collected birth histories for all women ages 15-50. A similar survey was undertaken in early 2001 covering essentially the same population studied in 1981; it also included some communities from farther north, near Lake Faguibine, where some people stayed in Mali during the rebellion but were internally displaced (see map, p. 4).

Most households who had transhumed into the delta in 1981 no longer go there, although some send their animals either with Bella (paid in cash or in kind) or with one or two family members. Whole household movements are now less common. This population now spends much or all of the year in the Mema. For a few, sedentarization in the Mema began before the 1985 drought, for others after the drought, and for the majority subsequent to repatriation (Randall and Giuffrida, 2003). Some remain semisedentary, based in a *site*[11] for part of the year but transhuming with animals to wet season pastures.

The population is still in a state of flux with respect to lifestyle. Some nomads since repatriation have just decided to sedentarize. Others, who had been sedentary, transhumed in 2000 and were becoming more mobile. Each site has satellite nomadic camps around it whose members are often related to those in the site and herding their animals.

The 2001 Survey

A total of 8,270 normally resident Kel Tamasheq were surveyed in three areas (Table 1). In the Mema, we attempted to get total coverage of the population present within a circumscribed area in late January and early February, when most people are grouped together. This population was chosen because they were the same groups who were covered in 1981; many people recalled the earlier survey.

The Daouna is a more pastoral zone further north. The populations there can trace kinship links with many groups in the Mema, and some who had lived in the Mema before the forced migration chose to be repatriated in the Daouna. We surveyed all the communities in a geographical subarea of the Daouna.

Five communities were also surveyed further north in the hills and dunes toward Lake Faguibine. These communities had been chosen for a linked, intensive anthropological study of the consequences of forced migration, because in this northerly zone, some people did not become refugees in the rebellion, choosing instead to hide in the mountains and desert

---

[11]*Site* is the term given to a fixed community of former nomads that has been recently formed. A "village" in Mali refers to a settlement with a particular administrative role. A few *sites* have now been granted village status.

TABLE 1 Population Characteristics, 1981, 2001

Characteristic	1981	2001
De jure population	6,125	8,270
Sex ratio	0.98	1.04
Tuareg (red)	1.07	1.06
Bella & blacksmiths (black)	0.88	0.96
Individual interviews	All women ages 15-50: 1,289 interviews 89 percent eligible women	Ever-married women ages 12-55: 1,313 interviews 79.1 percent eligible women Ever-married men: 739 interviews 54.7 percent eligible men
Tuareg proportion of population	0.53	0.765

with their animals (this was not possible in the flat open landscapes further south).[12] They are all related to people in the Mema and the Daouna, and many in these northern communities also have close kinship links with the Tuareg social, political, and intellectual elite.

All the sites were identified by locally knowledgeable people and on arrival in each site the team presented itself and its aims. It explained carefully the units of enumeration (*ejedesh* = household or dependents, larger than the tent used in 1981) and emphatically disassociated itself from the government administration, which might have led to underenumeration, and from all NGOs, which could have led to inflation of households and children because of perceived extra per capita distributions. Kinship relationships between the population and both the driver and the interviewers often facilitated trust and cooperation.

Lists of household heads included information on nearby nomadic camps using the site's well. Household questionnaire information was ob-

---

[12]One nomadic camp in the anthropological study refused to participate in the demographic survey.

tained from an adult member of the household. Individual questionnaires for all ever-married women and men were done with the respondents themselves, including marriage histories, birth histories, and knowledge about contraception. Problems in working with a mobile population rendered such individual questionnaires difficult to administer. People—particularly men but also women—moved continuously. They were away visiting, at market, herding animals, working, collecting water, and many were sick. Ideally one would wait to interview them later, but many sites and camps were small—often two to four households—and several such camps might be covered by the team in one day. It was not feasible to wait around for people to return or to revisit later; we had only one car and limited time and most camps were well away from any roads. Thus for absentees, data on children ever born, surviving children, and number of marriages were collected from other members of the household. Such summary data were also collected for women over age 55 because their birth and marriage histories were found to be too time-consuming and inaccurate.

Thus some of the fertility data analyzed below are an amalgam of these two different sources of data, whereas detailed birth history and marriage data are from the subsection of men and women who were interviewed. They can be considered a random choice of individuals from within their age group. The age distributions are very similar but with slightly higher proportions of middle-aged men (40-49) and women (35-44) with individual interviews. A comparison of marital status, parity, and reported proportions of children dead between the women interviewed and not interviewed indicates no significant differences between the two groups.

Dates and Ages

A major problem for a demographer with this population is its almost total lack of interest in chronological time and ages. Although the few who were educated had a good knowledge of event dates, the vast majority had difficulty even recalling the year. We developed an annual event calendar (itself complicated by the fact that named Tamasheq years run from wet season to wet season, approximately July to July). Still, there were substantial numbers of people who could not name the years of birth of their children, at times being unable to recall whether they were born before or after key events in the rebellion. A few birth histories were impossible to reconcile with the stated events. There was no point trying to determine month of birth: Islamic months shift each year, and many people recalled only Ramadan and Eid, with few knowing the Tamasheq names of other months. Women were better at recalling season of birth, particularly for births that occurred while they were nomadic, because they could recall where they were at the birth and thus deduce the season. For these reasons, although substantial effort was made to get accurate ages, all data on timing are fairly imprecise, which is unfortunate when trying to document the impact of traumatic circumstances on demographic events. A 3-year running mean is sometimes used below to examine time trends, since this seems the most appropriate way of dealing with lack of precision about event timing combined with random fluctuations of relatively rare events.

Disorder and Disruption

From the birth histories (from women ages 15-55), we estimated year of birth. Other work on pastoralists (Leslie and Fry, 1989) suggests that there is likely to be substantial annual fluctuation as a consequence of ecological conditions. Along with relatively small numbers and reporting errors, this means that we expected the data to be uninterpretable. However, from annual births (Figure 2) there is evidence of a deficit of births during the period of disorder, and the decline in the number of births relative to the fitted line occurs in 1992. The scale of this fertility decline is small and similar for both those who went to the refugee camps and those who remained nomadic during the crisis. For this population at least, the brake on fertility was only temporary and slight, and it was totally compensated for by the rebound over the next two years.

In a period of disorder it might be expected that the probability of a birth ending in stillbirth or miscarriage could rise due to trauma and poor conditions. Figure 3 documents the proportions of all reported birth events that were either stillbirths or miscarriages for the total population and for those who were in the refugee camps between 1991 and 1996; the numbers are very small. Stillbirths did peak in 1991, the year of flight, but then declined annually during the refugee camp period. This could be a function of the maternity services provided in the refugee camps, which occasionally included emergency evacuations for caesarians. Such maternity care is no longer available since repatriation, and the stillbirth rate has increased. The miscarriage distribution is less clear, with no evidence that the disorder period led to an increase in miscarriages for the overall population. The limbo period of exile shows a pattern similar to that of stillbirths, with a gradual decline followed by an increase during repatriation.

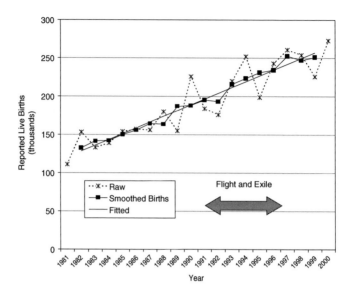

FIGURE 2 Annual reported live births: Raw data, smooth and fitted-total population.

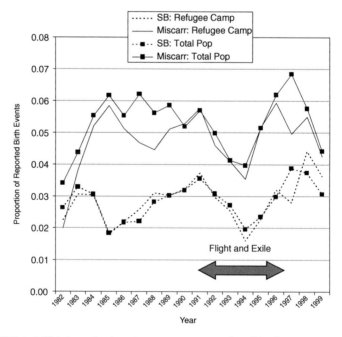

FIGURE 3 Stillbirths and miscarriages as proportion of total birth events: Smoothed using 3-year running mean.

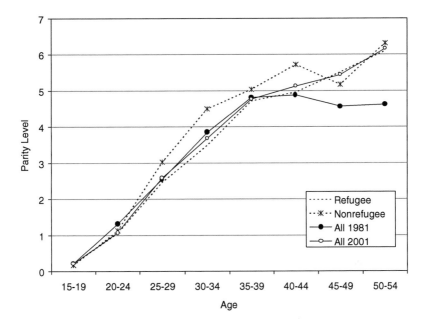

FIGURE 4 Parity by age, 1981 and 2001, by refugee status.

FERTILITY: PRECRISIS, DISORDER, LIMBO, AND NEW ORDER

Given problems with data quality for this population, especially ages and precise timing of events, it is appropriate to use as many different approaches as possible in order to assess the impact of forced migration on fertility. The most robust measure of fertility is reported parity by age, which for the total population is almost identical in 2001 to 1981 (Figure 4) up to age 40, after which there was poor reporting in 1981. This is extraordinary when one considers the substantial social, economic, and political changes in the intervening 20 years, along with a decline in childhood mortality from about 340 per 1,000 in the late 1970s to about 220[13] per 1,000 in the years preceding 2001. Tamasheq women now end their reproductive lives with substantially more surviving children than in 1981. A simple disaggre-

---

[13]Estimates made using Brass indirect methods. Direct methods give rather lower mortality, suggesting omission of dead children but still show substantial decline.

gation of the total population in 2001 into those who went to the refugee camps and those who did not indicates that people whose experience of the rebellion and forced migration differed also have higher reported parity by age.

Using the birth histories, it is possible to measure retrospective total fertility and age-specific fertility rates for different time periods and to combine these with measures from the 1981 survey. Several provisos are necessary. Year of birth was estimated from completed years since birth and season of birth, but birth details are available only for the 79 percent of ever-married women who provided birth histories. Because household-level data are available for all unmarried women, in order to calculate appropriate person-years at risk for the unmarried population, a sample of unmarried women was randomly selected from the household file with proportions matched by age, refugee, and social status with the proportions of ever-married women interviewed. The age data for the 1981 survey are much poorer than those for 2001, and we also know that neonatal mortality was underreported in that survey.

Combining the two data sets, age-specific fertility rates for 5-year periods from 1971 onward show little sign of any systematic trend in fertility over time, save a slight secular decline for younger women (Figure 5).[14] There is no evidence of changing fertility behavior at older ages.

Although useful for considering any overall trends, these 5-year periods are not particularly appropriate for examining the impact of forced migration. For that purpose, the following periods (which allow for a lag of 9 months for pregnancy) were preferred:

1985-1991: Prerebellion after the 1984-1985 drought.
1992-1993: Disorder: Early period in refugee camps; internal
            displacement and hiding for many nonrefugees.

---

[14]The apparently high age-specific fertility for women ages 35-39 (1981-1985) and 40-44 (1986-1990) is probably a combination of selectivity, age misreporting, and small numbers. These women were the oldest of those interviewed in 2001, many claimed to be too old to remember anything, and several interviews had to be abandoned. Many women genuinely seem to age very rapidly, possibly as a result of their harsh lifestyle as well as social expectations. With some notable exceptions, older women (and 45 was seen to be old) were thought to be beyond remembering details. Determining age was difficult for these women and thus exaggeration of ages is likely, which would lead to the apparently higher fertility when they were younger.

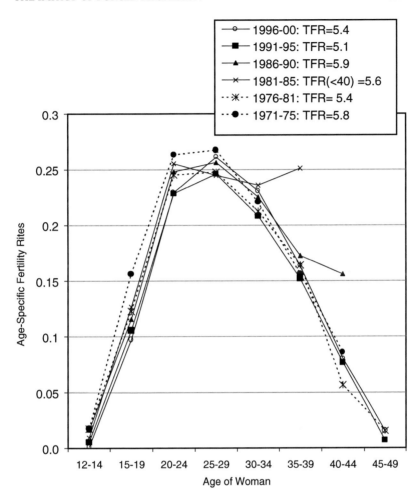

FIGURE 5 Age-specific fertility rates by period: Total population using 2001 and 1981 birth history data.

1994-1997: Limbo: Late period in refugee camps + repatriation; internal displacement and hiding for many nonrefugees.
1998-2000: New order: After repatriation.

People who declared that they spent at least 6 months in a refugee camp were defined as refugees. All others were classified as nonrefugees, yet it is important to note that most nonrefugees were also substantially af-

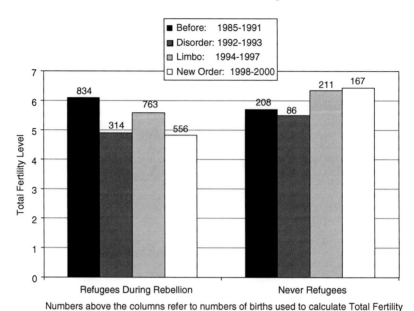

FIGURE 6 Total fertility: Refugees and nonrefugees by stage of forced migration.

fected by the rebellion. Some fled to Mauritania but never entered the refugee camps, others (including a few civil servants who became nomadic pastoralists again) retreated with their animals to extremely isolated areas in Mali, hidden from the army and militias. Many Bella fled to villages or urban areas in Mali, where life was more secure. Since 1997, all the refugees have been repatriated and many communities (especially the more northerly ones) include a mixture of ex-refugees and nonrefugees.

Figure 6 compares the total fertility rates (TFRs) of the two populations. Before the rebellion, those who were to become refugees had slightly higher TFRs than those who were not. During the disorder, fertility declined markedly for the refugees and insignificantly for the nonrefugees (despite the fact that many were internally displaced). For both groups, once the period of disorder was over, fertility rose somewhat (the rebound observed in Figure 2). Overall, during the whole rebellion period (1992-1997) total fertility declined for the refugees (TFR = 5.4) and increased slightly for nonrefugees (TFR = 6.1). This trend has become more marked since repatriation, with fertility declining further for the refugees and rising further for the nonrefugees.

Marriage

In 1981 the key proximate determinant of fertility that distinguished Kel Tamasheq from other rural Malian populations was their marriage regime, which had a substantial impact on fertility (Randall and Winter, 1985; Fulton and Randall, 1988). Marriage is the proximate determinant over which a noncontracepting population has most control. Entry into marriage, marital breakup, and possibly the initiation of innovative marital behavior are likely consequences of four of the forces identified in Figure 1 linking forced migration with fertility outcomes: biosocial, psychological, socioeconomic, and the political economy. In 1981 the largely monogamous Kel Tamasheq had low proportions of women currently married, a nonnegligible number of women who never married (around 5 percent), a relatively young age at first marriage for women, as well as a considerable amount of variability, a high frequency of divorce and widowhood, and substantial spousal age differences. Figure 7 shows that these patterns were maintained in 2001, but those who had been refugees had somewhat lower proportions married at most ages compared with the nonrefugees.

Why those who had been in refugee camps should have later ages at marriage and a higher percentage of widows and divorcees at older ages is not clear. It is unlikely to be a function of lack of available men, as there was no obvious sex or age bias in those who had been to the refugee camps. Also, since repatriation, the refugee and nonrefugee communities are intermixed, with women having access to the same pool of men. There is no evidence of an increase in informal unions while in the refugee camps. For Tuareg (but not for Bella) people, extramarital conceptions are socially unacceptable, although romantic liasons without penetrative sex are frequent. Despite rumors about illegitimate children, there was no evidence of them or, if they existed, that there were significant numbers of them. There is evidence from the anthropological study that the refugee camp experience with new contacts, new independence, and exposure to different ideas has eroded the traditional obedience of many younger women to their parents' marriage plans. Qualitative data suggest that girls and young women are now less likely to obey their parents meekly and marry when told. In several cases, young women refused to marry suitors proposed by their families. The social change fostered by the refugee camp experience may be an important aspect of change in entrance into marriage and remarriage.

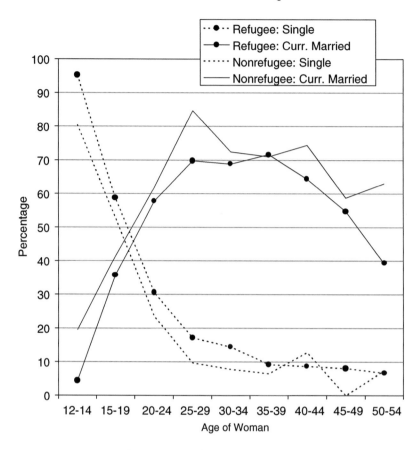

FIGURE 7 Percentage of women currently married and single by refugee status: Household data.

Marriage During the Disorder and Limbo Periods

Tamasheq marriage is based on exchanges of bride wealth and preferred marriage with close kin, especially any type of first cousin. In a time of disorder and flight, planned marriages are likely to be postponed temporarily or even permanently. It is also possible that there may be an increase in divorces and certainly in widowhood if the crisis is violent. Once people are established in refugee camps, provided that the food supply is ensured (which it was in this case) and that the population contains an adequate supply of both men and women, a range of factors may serve to stimulate marriages: boredom, a need for distraction, contact with a large number of new young people, and a perceived need to create new alliances and reinforce old ones. When marriage demands a certain number of prerequisites provided by both sides of the family (bride wealth and dowry), this may be an economic constraint to contracting new marriages. Evidence from a visit to the Tamasheq refugee camps in 1992 and from discussions in the field indicates that, during the exile, bride wealth was reduced to the nominal minimum stipulated by Islam and therefore would not have been a constraint on marriage.

Data from marital histories from the 79 percent of ever-married women of reproductive age include age at marriage (or year of marriage), kinship relationship with husband, the number of years together, the reason for the dissolution of the marriage, and the period until remarriage. Although the problems of dating outlined above apply, it is possible to estimate the year of marriage or dissolution. The same random sample of unmarried women used to calculate person-years at risk for fertility was used to generate a data set of representative women of reproductive age, from which one can measure approximate probabilities of different marital events by year. These are presented in Figure 8 using smoothed data (3-year running mean), since this is the most appropriate way of coping with both dating problems and small numbers of events.

Three marriage rates were considered: first marriages, remarriage of divorcees, and remarriage of widows. Figure 8 (comparing the total population and the subset who were in the refugee camps)[15] shows that the flight and refugee camp period did not appear to have a major impact on marriage dynamics. First marriage rates declined slightly in the early refugee camp period, whereas remarriage rates increased, only to decline later in the exile period and on repatriation.

Figure 9, which combines both sets of rates and compares refugees with nonrefugees, demonstrates that since the rebellion the refugees have consistently had lower marriage rates than nonrefugees, despite the fact

---

[15]We have no details on exactly when each individual entered and left the refugee camps, although the anthropological study indicates that some people from the northern areas did not flee until 1994. It is impossible to capture the complexity of movements in a single-round survey. Individuals were asked whether they spent at least 6 months in the refugee camps, on the assumption that for pastoral nomads it was time in the refugee camps that would have most impact on their behavior. Most people who replied "yes" to this question probably spent much of the 1991-1996 period in the camps.

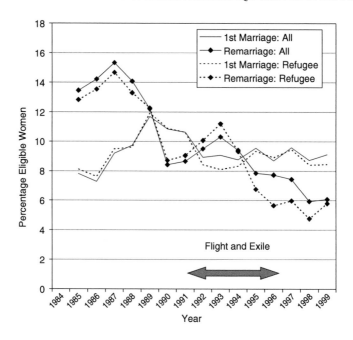

FIGURE 8 Annual (smoothed) first and remarriage rates: Refugees and all Tamesheq.

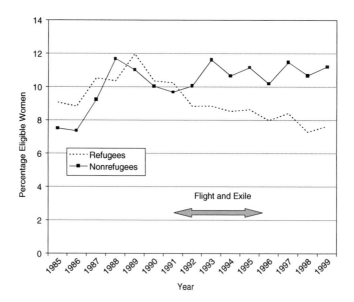

FIGURE 9 Smoothed annual all marriage rates: Refugees and nonrefugees.

that since 1997 they have all been living in the same communities. The decrease in marriages rates does not square with the perception of the refugee camp population, who said that marriages and the associated festivities were frequent. This is likely to be a misperception of denominators (as observed by Montgomery, 1998, in Nigeria for mortality): the large numbers of people in the refugee camps certainly meant that people were able to attend more weddings than in the dispersed precrisis small communities. They were a major form of entertainment for teenagers and young adults.

Marital Dissolution

Crisis can also impact marital dissolution. Widowhood will increase if there are substantial fatalities, and it is likely that divorce will also be affected. Kel Tamasheq divorce easily and for diverse reasons—lack of respect, insulting the in-laws, economic stress, marital disputes, apparently even as a way for the husband to demonstrate how much he loves his wife.[16] The practice of monogamy means that if a man wants to marry someone else, he has to divorce his current wife. It was predicted that divorce rates might decline during the period of disorder because people were preoccupied with more life-threatening issues, and as the limbo period progressed, divorce rates might rise, but there were no obvious trends in either divorce or widowhood. Still, in the raw data (not shown), 1991 stands out as having fewer divorces and new widows than other years for the refugee population.

Despite the small numbers, it is interesting to note that for both divorce and widowhood the greatest divergence between the refugees and nonrefugees occurs during the forced migration period, seen more clearly when comparing the refugee population with the total population studied (Figure 10), with refugees having more divorces and fewer widows. Overall, the period of flight and exile appears to have had only a minor effect on marriage rates in this population. The lack of substantial disruption can be seen as an indicator of the robustness of the structures that maintain biological and social reproduction.

---

[16]Through the suffering he is prepared to undergo by not being married to her. There were also people who said they didn't know why they had divorced.

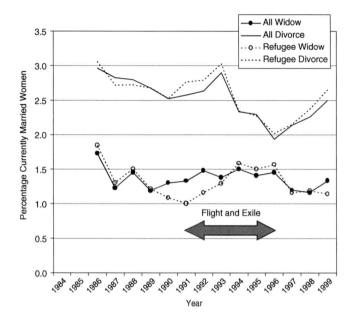

FIGURE 10 Annual marriage dissolution rates (smoothed): All Tamesheq and refugees.

Multivariate Analysis of Fertility by Period

The fertility differences observed above do suggest a divergence between those who were refugees and those who were not, at least in the period since repatriation, with more nonrefugees being currently married (Figure 7). The sociodemographic composition of the nonrefugee population differs from those who fled to the refugee camps. Nonrefugees include more Bella and blacksmiths and more people from the northern communities, where education levels are higher and there are closer kinship links with the political elite. Multivariate analysis was undertaken to determine whether there was an independent role of refugee camp residence on fertility and whether this was mediated through marriage.

Although in theory residence is time variant, complexities of movement meant that we collected information only on the dominant mode of life during a particular period rather than a complete migration history. Thus all individuals were either refugees (having spent at least 6 months in a refugee camp) or nonrefugees. A lag to allow for the 9 months of pregnancy was built into the model by using 2-year time periods that start in 1992 (whereas the rebellion and the first flights started in April-May 2001). Two sets of models were constructed in which the outcome variable was having a live birth during the 2-year period:[17] the first included all women regardless of their marital status and the second used only currently married women. Women who were at least age 12 at the beginning of the 2-year period were included. A variable representing the educational environment of the household was constructed, coded 1 if the household included an educated adult over age 20 other than the woman herself. This variable led to the exclusion of 60 women from the analysis whose data were collected when they were visiting another community and who therefore could not be linked with their household. Since this variable was never significant, it was excluded, and all women were included in the analyses.

The following variables are used in the multivariate logistic regression (completed using the forward conditional procedure in SPSS):

CEBt	Children ever born at time t – the year before the start of the period examined.
LCt	Living Children at time t – the year before the start of the period.
Age and age squared	Age in 2001.
Refugee status	Refugee spent more than 6 months in a refugee camp.
Literacy	Whether the woman herself was literate in either French or Arabic.
Status	Tuareg or Bella/blacksmith.

All the regressions were undertaken for all women, ever-married women (not shown), and currently married women in order to establish whether fertility differentials were caused by variation in nuptiality (Table 2).

---

[17]In the rare case in which a woman gave birth twice in the 2-year period, only one birth was counted.

TABLE 2 Odds Ratios of Giving Birth in 2-Year Periods

| Births in Period | All Women (Married and Unmarried) | | | |
	1992-1993 Disorder	1994-1995 Limbo	1996-1997 Late Limbo and Repatriation	1998-1999 New Order
N women	1,248	1,383	1,541	1,678
constant	−13.908 ***	−12.817 ***	−13.043 ***	−9.333 ***
CEB_t	1.362 ***	1.442 ***	ns	1.365 ***
LC_t	ns	ns	1.408 ***	ns
age (in 2001)	2.252 ***	2.196 ***	2.329 ***	1.853 ***
agesq	0.988 ***	0.987 ***	0.986 ***	0.989 ***
Refugee status refugee = reference	1.439 *	ns	1.442 *	1.349 *
Status (Tuareg = reference)	ns	ns	ns	ns
Literacy	ns	ns	ns	ns
	Currently Married Women			
N women	687	753	826	906
constant	−4.495 *	−5.184 **	−7.138 ***	−4.062 ***
CEB_t	1.131 *	1.184 ***	ns	1.153 ***
LC_t	ns	ns	1.158 **	ns
age (in 2001)	1.4202 **	1.460 ***	1.708 ***	1.387 ***
agesq	0.9940 ***	.993 ***	0.991 ***	0.993 ***
Refugee status refugee = reference	1.583 *	ns	ns	ns
Status (Tuareg = ref)	ns	ns	1.561 *	1.461 *
Literacy	ns	ns	ns	ns

$* = p < 0.05 \ ** \ p < 0.01 \ ***p < 0.001$.

From these models it is clear that having been a refugee did influence Kel Tamasheq fertility but that the proximate determinants changed during the different stages of the forced migration process. During the disorder of flight, the fertility of refugees was reduced relative to that of nonrefugees, both for all women and for the currently married, suggesting, as indicated in the framework (Figure 1), that biological processes, probably stress, spousal separation, and loss of libido were the major determinants rather than differential nuptiality. In the relatively stable limbo period, when life in the refugee camps was established and stress was much reduced, there was no difference in the odds ratios of giving birth between refugees and nonrefugees. In the late limbo period, which for the refugee population

included the element of new disorder during repatriation[18] —the odds ratios of all nonrefugee women giving birth increased relative to refugees, but
this time nuptiality rather than biological proximate determinants was the
most important factor, since refugee status did not have a significant impact on the odds ratios for married women. At this stage, social status differentials appear, with the odds of married Bella women giving birth being
significantly higher than those of Tuareg women. The pattern of differential nuptiality between refugees and nonrefugees impacting fertility was
maintained in 1998-1999 in the new order after repatriation, as was the
apparently greater fecundity of married Bella women (most of whom were
not refugees).

Thus although the total fertility time trends (Figure 5) suggest a
sociopolitical impact of flight on fertility (through longer term divergent
trends for refugees and nonrefugees), the multivariate analysis indicates that
this was probably largely a biological and biosocial response at times of
movement and stress rather than a behavioral response to refugee camp
residence. It must be remembered that those who did not reside in the
refugee camps were also severely affected by the rebellion in terms of stress
and persecution; the majority were either internally or externally displaced,
just not in refugee camps. Even Bella and blacksmiths, who were rarely
persecuted, were affected by the conflict in Mali and, along with many of
the non-Tamasheq population, abandoned their camps and villages to move
to other, more secure areas.

Toward the end of the conflict, in the late limbo and the new order
periods, different patterns of nuptiality emerged that impacted fertility.
Many aspects of Tuareg marriage can be interpreted as consequent to both
socioeconomic and psychological changes engendered by the exile and as
part of strategies by individuals and groups to consolidate social links. The
aspects of nuptiality that have most impact on fertility are clearly age at first
marriage, proportions marrying, and remarriage rates after marital dissolution, since these aspects of the regime influence the absolute numbers of
women married and therefore exposed to births. As we saw earlier, the
nonrefugees had both an earlier age at marriage (Figure 7), higher propor-

---

[18]Accounts of the repatriation suggest that leaving the sheltered refugee camps was very
stressful for many people. Often the promised infrastructure in Mali was unavailable, and the
rations and other provisions were often perceived to be inadequate. Water supplies were
particularly problematic in some sites.

tions married, and higher marriage rates (Figure 9); in the case of the latter, it appears that refugee marriage rates have declined, rather than there being an increase for nonrefugees.

Female education is not a determinant of fertility in this population, largely because levels of education are so low. The proportions of all women of reproductive age who were literate rose from 2.3 percent in 1992-1993 to 3.8 percent in 1998-1999 (an increase of 29 to 64 women). This increase in female literacy is definitely a consequence of the exile and the schools that were set up in the refugee camps. Most of the literate women in 1998-1999 were still very young, and it is at present unclear whether their education will affect their nuptiality and fertility.

Although refugee camp residence appears to have had little impact on overall fertility during the limbo period, it is likely that the dramatically altered lifestyle conditions in the camps for the previously nomadic women influenced marital behavior and contraceptive knowledge. This presumably would occur through increased social contact with large numbers of people, as well as contact with modern health services. This experience may have longer term repercussions for fertility, not observable in this relatively short time frame.

Age at Marriage and Choice of Spouse

In addition to the gross rates of marriage and marital dissolution, marital behavior may change in more subtle ways, reflecting the impact of exile on a population's identity and perception of itself relative to others. Age at first marriage and choice of spouse are factors that come to mind.

In 1981 age at first marriage was very poorly reported. I have more confidence in the retrospective reports of age at marriage for the 2001 data. These allow examination of age at marriage for different time periods, although for the earlier time periods the data are biased by the age structure of the sample, which becomes progressively younger as it is projected back in time. Because determinants of marriage in terms of bride wealth, choice of spouse, and political and economic motives for marrying are very different for Bella and Tuareg[19] (Randall and Winter, 1985), I focus here just on

---

[19]They are also different for blacksmiths, for whom class endogamy and a relatively small pool of potential spouses mean that patterns of age at marriage and kinship relationships are very particular.

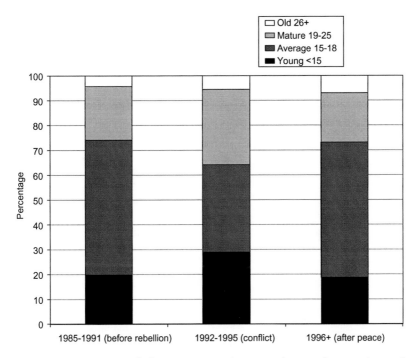

FIGURE 11 Percentage of all Tuareg women by reported age at first marriage and period of marriage.

the Tuareg. They were the most affected by the rebellion and their distribution of age at first marriage (Figure 11) clearly differs during the rebellion period (chi squared p = 0.005), returning to the previous pattern after repatriation (the increase in the proportion of marriages over age 26 is just a function of the changing age structure of women reporting).

Breaking down the population into the refugees and nonrefugees (Figure 12)[20] shows that those who subsequently became refugees and those who did not had almost identical distributions of age at first marriage before 1985, although age at first marriage did diverge *before* the forced migration. In the six years preceding the rebellion, those who did not become refugees had fewer older and very young marriages. During the conflict, more refugee camp marriages were of young girls, whereas outside the

---

[20]All marriages over age 19 are combined to remove cells with small counts.

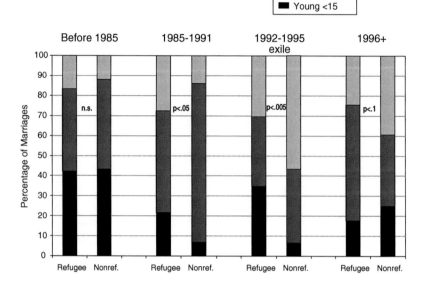

FIGURE 12 Percentage of Tuareg women by reported age at first marriage, period of marriage and refugee status.

camps older women were much more likely to be married (chi squared $p < 0.005$). Since repatriation, the distribution of refugee women's age at first marriage has reverted toward the prerebellion behavior, and both groups are tending to converge.

It is hard to interpret the trend of marrying off older women among those who were not refugees (many of whom were internally displaced and hiding in remote areas), unless it was an intention to provide protection at a difficult time. For those in the refugee camps, the increase in young marriages can be seen as a consequence of two trends: first, the active social life that young people led in the refugee camps, with substantially increased peer groups and parties that went on for days, may have led parents to want to protect their daughters through marriage.[21] Second, there may have been political motives: the grouping of substantial numbers of people with little

---

[21]There are stories that there was a substantial increase in premarital pregnancies, although none was reported in the survey, possibly because they were seen as very shameful.

to do except discuss strategies for the future is likely to have led men to organize marriages that might create useful future alliances, an important aspect of Tamasheq arranged marriages.

Choice of spouse is a further aspect of marriage that may have little impact on reproductive health and fertility, but it affects infant mortality and also contributes to understanding how a population adapts to forced migration. Tamasheq have long preferred close kin marriage and social class endogamy. Although no data are available on spousal kinship relationships from 1981,[22] the 2001 marriage histories can be used retrospectively to examine spousal relationship patterns. Data on the relationship between husband and wife[23] are very reliable, since kinship is a major conversational preoccupation of Tamasheq women. Only the closest relationship was recorded,[24] which underestimates levels of consanguinity, since people can usually trace their kinship relationship through several different lines. Overall about 60 percent of marriages are between second cousins or closer (Figure 13).

It was hypothesized that in the refugee camps increased contacts with a wider social circle would lead to more marriages among nonkin, which was not observed. In fact, there was no significant change in the distribution of marriages by kin during the rebellion; the changes have occurred since repatriation and only for remarriage ($p = 0.001$), with a near doubling of first cousin remarriages. Patterns of kin marriages did not change significantly for the refugees in any period, but nonrefugees have been more likely to marry close kin since repatriation ($p = 0.054$) than before. This move toward more close kin marriages, especially in second marriages in which spouses have more choice, suggests that the population may be turning in upon itself when faced with wider tensions with other populations. Increased levels of consanguineous marriage may also be a consequence of the

---

[22]Qualitative data collected at that time indicate that close kin marriages were very frequent and preferred by most people.

[23]Tamasheq distinguish between patrilateral parallel cousins, matrilateral parallel cousins, and cross-cousins. They also know the number of generations since the common ancestor (first, second, third cousins, etc). Data were collected on the relationship using the Tamasheq terminology to avoid confusion.

[24]Because of multiple kinship links caused by generations of close kin marriage, many couples could choose between different relationships: that is, they may have been both first-generation patrilateral cousins and second-generation matrilateral cousins. They were asked for the closest relationship, but there may have been a reporting bias toward preferred patrilateral relationships.

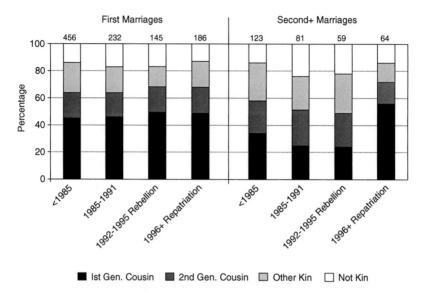

FIGURE 13 Kinship distance of Tuareg marriages: Distribution over time for first and subsequent marriages.

wider political process of decentralization and the new political alliances and allegiances that it is entailing.

In 1981 marriage was the proximate determinant of fertility, which made the Tamasheq fertility regime different from other rural Malians. If fertility were to be significantly affected by forced migration, then nuptiality changes were the most likely driving force. To a degree this was observed in the later period of the conflict and after repatriation, although more among the nonrefugees than the refugees. In this population nonrefugees (particularly the Tuareg) were affected substantially by the rebellion in their daily lives—some living in exile but not in refugee camps, others being internally displaced in Mali. The analysis suggests that it is essential to consider all those affected by a crisis and not just the visible population sheltered in refugee camps and the forced migrants outside the country. Certainly the more subtle nuptiality responses were more marked among these internally displaced individuals with changing age at first marriage and increased endogamy, with the latter impact *after* repatriation, during the new order. In terms of the impact on child mortality, differences in survivorship between children of closely related parents and more distantly related parents have been very significant in the past four years, indicating that these changing marriage patterns may have demographic repercussions other than just on fertility.

Use of Contraception

No data are available on contraception in 1981 because pilot tests indicated both no knowledge of contraception and that questions on the topic were likely to cause significant problems. Simplified questions in the style of Demographic and Health Surveys on knowledge and use of contraception were asked in 2001, but they were often unwelcome.[25] We have a strong suspicion that some women had knowledge that they did not admit to about some methods—in particular, withdrawal.[26]

Qualitative data indicate that contraception was available in the refugee camps and that publicity campaigns made people aware of family planning methods. Reports were contradictory, with some women stating that such campaigns were prominent and others denying all knowledge of either the campaigns or contraception. Because of their wider experience and contacts, we expected those who had been in the refugee camps to have more knowledge and higher levels of use than nonrefugee women. Of 1,110 women interviewed, only 17 had ever used modern contraception, 22 admitted to using traditional methods (mainly rhythm and withdrawal), and 4 of them had used both. Although such small numbers do not allow for much examination, bivariate analysis shows that being literate in either Arabic or French or having ever lived in a town or village was associated with both modern and traditional fertility control (chi squared $p < 0.001$), whereas neither social class nor residence in a refugee camp had any association with fertility control. Women of all age groups had used modern contraception, but behavioral methods were more associated with younger

---

[25]We abandoned asking the questions of postmenopausal women after about 8 communities: 60 (4.5 percent) women refused to answer and 31 weren't asked because they lived in a community in which we were warned that we would be asked to leave if we mentioned such things.

[26]One enumerator, who had lived in several of these communities as well as in the refugee camps, commented that most young women know about and may use coitus interruptus in both premarital and extramarital relationships (but never within marriage). She was surprised how few admitted to knowing about it.

women. Such low levels of contraceptive use will have no impact on population levels of fertility.

Knowledge About Contraception

In contrast to the situation regarding use of contraception, more women knew about contraception, and such knowledge was probably underrecorded (see footnote 25). Few women spontaneously described methods, but many more were able to recognize methods described to them. Most of those women who admitted knowing modern methods also knew traditional methods (Table 3), suggesting that embarrassment or shame at declaring any knowledge was overcome once some knowledge was admitted. From the bivariate analysis of contraceptive knowledge (Table 4) by

TABLE 3 Percentage Ever-Married Women Knowing Different Contraceptive Methods (Spontaneous and Prompted)

Number of Methods	Modern Methods	Behavioral (Withdrawal and Rhythm)	Traditional (Grisgris and Plants)	Any Method
0	56.7%	82.6%	81.3%	54.0%
1	10.7	12.6	16.3	8.9
2	13.7	4.8	2.4	9.9
3+	18.9	na	na	27.2

N = 1,110

TABLE 4 Significance of Bivariate Analysis of Knowledge About Contraceptive Methods (2 by 2 Tables and Fisher's Exact Test)

	Modern	Behavioral	Traditional	Any Method
Has lived in town or village	**	***	***	**
Literate in Arabic or French	***	***	***	***
In refugee camp	*	ns	ns	ns
Tuareg	**	ns	ns	*

* = p < 0.05 ** p < 0.01 ***p < 0.001

individual characteristics, the refugee camps appear to have played little role in disseminating information, except possibly knowledge about modern contraception. This is confirmed by the multivariate analysis (see Tables 5 and 6), in which having lived in a refugee camp had no impact on the odds of knowing about any form of fertility control. Those who have been nomadic since repatriation were less likely to know about modern or traditional contraception (but not behavioral). Women in households in which there was a literate adult were more likely to know about both modern and behavioral methods but not traditional ones. The largest and most significant odds ratio was for literate women—which is to be expected, but given the tiny number of such women (31), the impact would be negligible.

Tuareg women were more likely than Bella to know about modern

TABLE 5 Number of Ever-Married, Nonmenopausal Women Who Were Asked and Responded to Contraceptive Knowledge Questions

Variable		N	% in Reference Category
Status	Tuareg (ref)	759	77.8
	Bella & blacksmiths	217	
Mobility	nomadic/seminomadic after repatriation (ref)	475	48.7
	sedentary after repatriation	501	
Litadult	no literate adult in household (ref)	862	88.3
	literate adult in household (excluding woman herself)	114	
Litwoman	woman illiterate (ref)	945	96.8
	literate French or Arabic	31	
Refugee	in refugee camp (ref)	787	80.6
	never in refugee camp	189	
Urbliv	never lived in village/town (ref)	868	88.9
	has lived in village or town	108	
Age group	age 30+ (ref)	458	46.9
	age under 30	518	

TABLE 6 Odds Ratios of Knowledge About Contraception Methods

Variable	Modern	Behavioral	Traditional	Any Method
Mobility	1.36 *	ns	1.57 *	1.37 *
Litadult	1.54 *	1.67 *	ns	1.53 *
Litwoman	4.25 **	3.32 **	3.05 **	3.89 **
Status	0.64 **	ns	ns	0.70 *
Urbliv	ns	1.71 *	2.28 ***	ns
CEB	ns	0.94 *	ns	ns
Refugee	ns	ns	ns	ns
Age group	ns	ns	ns	ns

* = $p < 0.05$ ** $p < 0.01$ ***$p < 0.001$
CEB = Children ever born.

contraception but not behavioral or traditional methods, whereas those who had ever lived in towns or villages (multiethnic populations with some health services) knew more about traditional and behavioral methods than those who had always lived only in Tamasheq camps or sites. Knowledge about any form of fertility control was unrelated to a woman's age.

With the exception of the lack of impact of refugee camps, these results are hardly surprising. However, a proviso must be added. The data are really measuring, not knowledge about fertility control, but rather a willingness to admit to that knowledge. This explains the impact of education (both of the woman and her household) and of living in a village or urban area. The interviewers were such women and often developed the best rapport with similar women. The strong ethos of shame in Tamasheq society, along with a belief that fertility control is contrary to Islamic law, means that many women would not admit to knowing about any form of fertility control, because such knowledge might reflect adversely on them. Education, contact with educated adults, and life in more cosmopolitan communities (which involves such contact) all tended to break down these traditional barriers and make the women more open to such conversations. All the interviewers felt strongly that many women were denying knowledge that they had, but it is not clear whether such denial was related to having lived in the refugee camps.

Although the process of the rebellion, forced migration, and refugee camp living were not apparently related to knowledge or use of contraception, one of the consequences of the forced migration was that a few former civil servants and city dwellers decided to abandon their urban jobs and come to live in rural communities after repatriation. The wives and daughters of these men made up a majority of both women who had lived in towns or villages and those who were literate: 45 percent of literate women had lived in villages or towns compared with 9 percent of illiterate women. Thus although residence in refugee camps may not have transformed knowledge, the sociopolitical consequences of the rebellion mean that a more heterogeneous female population now lives in the rural areas, mainly in the sedentarized sites, and they may well influence reproductive behavior in the near future.

Other Proximate Determinants of Fertility

Other proximate determinants of fertility were considered, but there seems to have been little change engendered by the forced migration. Levels of primary sterility among younger currently married women were slightly higher than in 1981 (and for both periods are higher than for Mali as a whole (République du Mali, 1996), but the increase is largely among the nonrefugee population, and the numbers are small (Figure 14).

Breast-feeding behavior does not seem to have altered—all women breast-fed, as in 1981—and ideally they wean at 24 months unless another pregnancy intervenes. No data are available on supplementation.

CONCLUSIONS

Despite mass forced migration, substantial social change (change in production, way of life, and loss of domestic slaves), and a prolonged period in refugee camps, the overall fertility of the Tamasheq has remained remarkably stable, with little observable difference between 1981 and 2001. This stability does mask more subtle changes in both fertility and marital behavior, most of which can be shown to be temporarily associated with either flight, residence in the refugee camps, or repatriation. This suggests that, for this particular population, the general stability may be a function of the fact that the crisis was not accompanied by large massacres and total social disorder. People fled to avoid this, and as such the flight was successful. Mobility is the normal response for this population to changing resource availability and the spatial and seasonal distribution of stress, the movement to the refugee camps and the tented accommodation in the camps did not represent a major change in physical living conditions. In

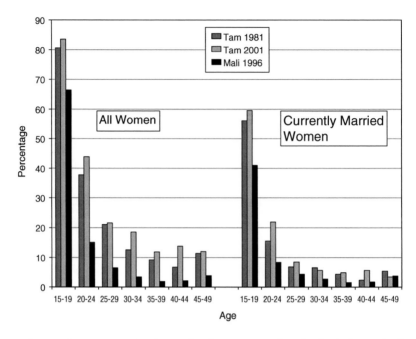

FIGURE 14 Percentage Tamasheq and Malian women with no live births by age (Mali data from 1996 DHS).

contrast, it was the lack of mobility once in the camps, the high population density, and the loss of livelihood and independence that was the fundamental disruption to them as well as a general improvement in health, education, and sanitation services and living in a much larger and more diverse local community.

This study was originally undertaken to focus on these socioeconomic and political changes and their impact on demographic behavior. It was thought that for a minority ethnic group with a traditionally dispersed population, a period of five years in densely populated refugee camps was likely to engender pronatalism and deliberate changes in fertility behavior. In 1981 the Tamasheq showed themselves to be very demographically aware—possibly because their literate leaders had read the colonial archives, which were often obsessed with Tamasheq demography and low fertility. They were conscious of the fact that their fertility was lower and their mortality higher than other Malian populations; they were already concerned about this in 1981. The 1981 study had shown that their low fertility and low growth rates were largely a consequence of monogamy, frequent divorce and widowhood, and, for reproductive-age women, long periods of being unmarried.

For a Muslim population, for whom polygamy is a theoretical option, such a situation would allow for the development of deliberate pronatalism that could easily be acted on; an increase in polygamy levels would allow a substantial increase in fertility. Pronatalist responses are not unheard of among displaced populations. The Palestinians have much higher fertility than would be expected for their educational achievement and general level of development, despite which, during the Intifada, they managed to increase already high fertility, especially in the Gaza Strip (Pedersen, Randall, and Khawaja, 2001) in response to pronatalist exhortations. However in the new order period for the Malian Kel Tamasheq, there is no evidence of such pronatalism nor of an increase in polygamy.

In order to draw lessons from the experience of this population in terms of understanding the impact of forced migration on reproduction, one needs to focus on the original temporal framework of disorder, limbo, and new order. Tamasheq fertility was temporarily disrupted during disorder, with a rebound (as in a famine) after conditions improved. Because the flight and the living conditions in the refugee camps did not represent a major break with preconflict lifestyle, the temporary disruption was slight, and it is likely that the more intense the disruption and disorder, the greater the impact on fertility. For the Tamasheq there was further slight disruption during repatriation, which in this case also included an element of disorder. The multivariate analysis indicates that the impact on fertility was due to nuptiality changes in that period rather than biological stresses, suggesting that this cannot be generalized to other populations who may not have such a flexible marriage regime as the Tamasheq. Overall, the gross fertility levels of the population have remained largely unchanged since 1981, and the new order is virtually indistinguishable from the old order.

Disaggregation of the population suggests that both the refugees and the nonrefugees were affected by the rebellion and the forced migration, but in different ways that are masked if one looks at the entire population. Subtle changes in rates of marital dissolution and in patterns of age at first marriage suggest social responses to the changing circumstances; these responses are even more marked for the nonrefugees (who were often internally and externally displaced) than for those who were in the refugee camps. The changing reproductive behavior of those who were not in the refugee camps is a constant theme, although as a relatively small proportion of the overall population, they have little overall impact on fertility dynamics.

Although it was predicted that the original characteristics of this population would mean that refugee camp residence would have a major impact on attitudes and behavior, it may be instead that the nomadic lifestyle, which most had lived before, meant that the continuity was more important than the transformation, at least in physical terms. Nomadism is, of course, very specific to this particular group and would be unlikely to apply to many other situations of forced migration.

For these Kel Tamasheq people, repatriation has had as much impact on reproductive behavior as the original crisis, with several indices of demographic well-being deteriorating since repatriation—such as stillbirth rates and the mortality differentials between children with related parents and those with unrelated parents. Estimates of maternal mortality suggest that this remains a huge reproductive health problem. Using the sisterhood method (Graham et al., 1989), the lifetime risk of a maternal death is estimated as 1 in 8, almost double the national level (République du Mali, 1996). As an indirect estimate, this cannot be disaggregated into refugees and nonrefugees, but it is certainly a major reproductive issue for both. Questions on ideal family size and intentions to use contraception, when they were taken seriously, often elicited the response that women wanted no children or would like to use contraception, not through any desire to limit numbers of children but because they were terrified of pregnancy and childbirth.

Although this case study does not demonstrate substantial fertility-related consequences of forced migration, it does allow consideration of the potential impact of other forced migration situations. First, the consequences on all aspects of reproduction will vary over the period of forced migration and according to the intensity of the crisis. Second, the reproduction of the internally displaced and nonrefugee population must be considered as well as that of the visible refugee population in camps. Social, political, and local environmental changes engendered by the crisis may differ for the two groups, but each has to protect its members and continue to reproduce itself. Precrisis reproductive strategies, which in this case were endogamy, marriage alliances, and reproductive behaviors intimately tied up with identity to the group, may be reinforced and entrenched to emphasize separateness from other groups; this may explain the particular changes observed in age at first marriage and spousal choice as well as the maintenance of monogamy, in which the economic costs and value of both women and children have changed significantly. Third, the consequences of forced migration for reproduction need to be considered at a range of different levels: biological, psychological, socioeconomic, and political. The social and demographic history of the population in an ecological and political environment are as much a part of the response to forced migration as the hardship, hunger, and spousal separation. That is why it is important to understand the story of the many individual populations in a national conflict, and why national pictures may frequently be distorted.

ACKNOWLEDGMENTS

The 1981 demographic survey of the delta Tamasheq was financed by the International Livestock Centre for Africa as part of its socioeconomic research program, directed by Jeremy Swift. Further work on Tamasheq demography in 1982 was financed by the Population Council. The Economic and Social Research Council funded the study of the demography of repatriated Tamasheq refugees (grant no. R000238184), which was undertaken in collaboration with the Institut Supérieur de Formation et Recherche Appliquée (ISFRA), Université du Mali, Bamako. Alessandra Giuffrida undertook the anthropological component of this study and provided valuable contributions to and comments on this paper.

REFERENCES

Agadjanian, V., and N. Prata
   2002 War, peace and fertility in Angola. *Demography* 39(2):215-231.
Agency for Co-operation and Research in Development, Oxfam, and Netherlands Organisation for International Development Co-operation
   1995 *Nord du Mali : De la tragedie à l'Espoir.* Bamako, Mali: Organisation for International Development Co-operation.
Ashton, B., K. Hill, J. Piazza, and R. Zeitz
   1984 Famine in China 1958-61. *Population and Development Review* 10(4):613-645.
Brass, W.
   1968 *The Demography of Tropical Africa.* Princeton, NJ: Princeton University Press.
Courbage, Y.
   1995 The population of Palestine. *Population: An English Selection* 7:210-220.
Dyson, T.
   1991 On the demography of South Asian famines (Parts I & II). *Population Studies* 45(1):5-25 and 45(2):279-297.
Fulton, D.J.R., and S. Randall
   1988 Households, women's roles and prestige as factors determining nuptiality and fertility differentials in Mali. Pp. 191-211 in J. Caldwell, A. Hill, and V. Hull (eds.), *Micro Approaches to Demographic Research.* London: Kegan Paul International.
Gallais, J.
   1975 *Pasteurs et Paysans du Gourma: La Condition Sahelienne.* Paris: Centre National de la Recherche Scientifique.
Graham, W., W. Brass, and R. Snow
   1989 Estimating maternal mortality: The sisterhood method. *Studies in Family Planning* 20(3):125-135.
Hill, A.G., and S. Randall
   1984 Différences géographiques et sociales dans la mortalité infantile et juvenile au Mali. *Population* 39(6).
Khawaja, M.
   2000 The recent rise in Palestinian fertility: Permanent or transient? *Population Studies* 54(3):331-346.
Leslie, P.W., and P. Fry
   1989 Extreme seasonality of births among nomadic Turkana pastoralists. *American Journal of Physical Anthropology* 79:103-115.
Lestaeghe, R. (ed.)
   1989 *Reproduction and Social Organisation in sub Saharan Africa.* Berkeley, CA: University of California Press.
Lindstrom, D.P., and B. Berhanu
   1999 The impact of war, famine and economic decline on marital fertility in Ethiopia. *Demography* 36(2):247-261.

Marty, A.
  1999   La division sédentaires-nomades. Le cas de la boucle du Niger au début de la
          période coloniale. Pp. 289-306 in L. Holtedahl, S. Gerrard, M.Z. Njeuma, and J.
          Boutrais (eds.), *Le Pouvoir du Savoir de l'Arctique aux Tropiques*. Paris: Karthala.
Médecins Sans Frontières
  1997   *Refugee Health: An Approach to Emergency Situations*. New York: MacMillan
          Education LTD.
Montgomery, M.R.
  1998   Learning and lags in mortality perceptions. Pp. 112-137 in *From Death to Birth:
          Mortality Decline and Reproductive Change*. National Research Council,
          Committee on Population, M.R. Montgomery and B. Cohen, eds. , Washington,
          DC: National Academy Press.
National Research Council
  2004   *War, Humanitarian Crises, Population Displacement, and Fertility: A Review of
          Evidence*. Kenneth Hill. Roundtable on the Demography of Forced Migration.
          Committee on Population, Division of Behavioral and Social Sciences and
          Education and Program on Forced Migration and Health at the Mailman School
          of Public Health of Columbia University. Washington, DC: The National
          Academies Press.
Pedersen, J., S. Randall, and M. Khawaja, eds.
  2001   *Growing Fast: The Palestinian Population in the West Bank and Gaza Strip*. (Fafo
          report no. 353.) Oslo: Fafo Institute for Applied Social Science.
Randall, S.
  1984   A Comparative Demographic Study of Three Sahelian Populations: Marriage and
          Childcare as Intermediate Determinants of Fertility and Mortality, PhD thesis,
          London University.
  1996   Whose reality? Local perceptions of fertility versus demographic analysis.
          Population Studies 50(2):221-234.
Randall, S., and A. Giuffrida
  2003   Forced Migration, Sedentarization and Social Change: Malian Kel Tamasheq.
          Paper presented at International Association for the Study of Forced Migration
          Biennial Conference, Chiang Mai, Thailand, January.
Randall, S., and M.M. Winter
  1985   The reluctant spouse and the illegitimate slave: Marriage, household formation
          and demographic behavior among Malian Kel Tamasheq. In A.G. Hill (ed.),
          Population Health and Nutrition in the Sahel. London: Kegan Paul International.
République du Mali
  1996   *Enquête Démographique et Santé, Mali 1995-96*. Bamako, Mali: Direction
          Nationale de la Statistique et de l'Informatique and Calverton, MD: Macro
          International.
Sperl, S.
  2000   *International Refugee Aid and Social Change in Northern Mali. New Issues in Refugee
          Research*. (Working Paper no. 22.) New York: United Nations High Commissioner
          for Refugees.
Watkins, S.C., and J. Menken
  1985   Famines in historical perspective. *Population and Development Review* 11(4):647-
          675.

ABOUT THE AUTHOR

Sara Randall has a BA in Anthropology and a PhD in Demography and is currently a Senior Lecturer in the Anthropology department at University College London. She first did research on Tamasheq demography for her PhD in 1981 and has worked extensively on the demography and health of mobile populations in Mali and Burkina Faso. Having also worked on Palestinian demography and developed an interest in the role of both forced migration and minority status on demographic behaviour, the particular experiences of Malian Kel Tamasheq in the rebellion and repatriation were an obvious research topic for the author. She has now developed a general research interest in the demographic consequences of conflict and forced migration particularly with respect to fertility and nuptiality.

From her extensive field-based experience in challenging remote and multi-ethnic situations she has developed methodological interests in the production and meaning of demographic data and has focused on combining qualitative and quantitative approaches. These allow a better appreciation of robust demographic measures and concepts as well as an increased understanding of the determinants of demographic behaviour, especially amongst minority and marginalised populations.

The **Committee on Population** was established by the National Academy of Sciences (NAS) in 1983 to bring the knowledge and methods of the population sciences to bear on major issues of science and public policy. The committee's work includes both basic studies of fertility, health and mortality, and migration and applied studies aimed at improving programs for the public health and welfare in the United States and in developing countries. The committee also fosters communication among researchers in different disciplines and countries and policy makers in government and international agencies.

The **Roundtable on the Demography of Forced Migration** was established by the Committee on Population of the National Academy of Sciences in 1999. The Roundtable's purpose is to serve as an interdisciplinary, nonpartisan focal point for taking stock of what is known about demographic patterns in refugee situations, applying this knowledge base to assist both policy makers and relief workers, and stimulating new directions for innovation and scientific inquiry in this growing field of study. The Roundtable meets yearly and has also organized a series of workshops (held concurrently with Roundtable meetings) on some of the specific aspects of the demography of refugee and refugee-like situations, including mortality patterns, demographic assessment techniques, and research ethics in complex humanitarian emergencies. The Roundtable is composed of experts from academia, government, philanthrophy, and international organizations.

Other Publications of the Roundtable on the Demography of Forced Migration

Psychosocial Concepts in Humanitarian Work with Children: A Review of the Concepts and Related Literature (2003)

Initial Steps in Rebuilding the Health Sector in East Timor (2003)

Malaria Control During Mass Population Movements and Natural Disasters (2003)

Research Ethics in Complex Humanitarian Emergencies: Summary of a Workshop (2002)

Demographic Assessment Techniques in Complex Humanitarian Emergencies: Summary of a Workshop (2002)

Forced Migration and Mortality (2001)